Summary

OF

Leadership in Turbulent Times

By Doris Kearns Goodwin

Dennis Braun

Copywrite (c) 2018

INTRODUCTION:

If you go into just about any bookshop, you'll find an abundance of books claiming to hold the secrets of how to become a great leader. Many of these books are speculative and/or consist of scattered anecdotes. Readers seeking a more empirically-grounded, systematic approach to understanding leadership will find relief in this summary.

Based on detailed biographies of four of the most transformational presidents in US history, this summary identifies some key factors in the development of leadership. By comparing and contrasting Abraham Lincoln, Theodore Roosevelt, Franklin Roosevelt and Lyndon Johnson, we'll see the similarities and differences between their paths to the White House. This, in turn, will allow us to discern what is and isn't required for someone to become a great leader. Along the way, we'll find answers to some of the crucial questions of leadership studies: Are great leaders made, or do they make themselves – and if so, how?

GREAT LEADERS CAN COME FROM VERY DIFFERENT BACKGROUNDS.

If great leaders were just the products of their circumstances, then we might expect their backstories to share certain key features. But when we look at the lives of the transformational presidents, we see they come from dramatically different backgrounds.

Born to an illiterate father who eked out a living on one dirt farm after another, Lincoln grew up in the backwoods of Illinois in a cabin that was initially doorless, floorless and bedless. When he was about nine years old, his father disenrolled him from school so he could work on the farm.

Lincoln then had to educate himself. He walked long distances across the countryside to borrow books from people, then read them in his few spare moments. He did this without external support; indeed, if he was caught reading when he was supposed to be working, his father would sometimes beat him and destroy his books.

Upon entering adulthood, Lincoln was basically a nobody. Striking out from home to make a fresh start in life, he settled in the town of New Salem, Illinois. Because of his height and shabby appearance, the townsfolk regarded the newcomer as a bit of a freak. Through his friendliness and good deeds, like chopping wood for widows, he eventually won them over, but it took months of building relationships to earn enough of a reputation to run for a seat in the Illinois state assembly, which marked the beginning of his political career.

Lincoln's lack of wealth, access to education, parental support and connections stand in stark contrast to the circumstances of

Theodore Roosevelt. He was born with a trust fund bequeathed to him by his grandfather, a banker, merchant and real estate mogul who was one of the five richest individuals in New York.

His father was a well-respected philanthropist who provided him with a rigorous formal education and access to an extensive family library. If there was a book he didn't already have, his father would help him procure it.

When Theodore Roosevelt reached early adulthood, he did not need to convince local citizens of his merit to enter politics. Thanks to the power already attached to his family's name, he was recruited to run for the state assembly of New York by the local Republican Party.

If two people from such disparate circumstances could both become transformative presidents, the keys to becoming a great leader must lie somewhere else than in one's background.

GREAT LEADERS CAN HAVE VERY DIFFERENT PERSONAL CHARACTERISTICS

Another place to look for the key to becoming a great leader might be shared personal characteristics. But the influential presidents under consideration suggest we look elsewhere. Their personal characteristics were as different as their backgrounds.

Franklin Roosevelt and Lincoln, for example, had drastically different temperaments. Growing up with loving parents who provided him with a warm, stable, peaceful and nurturing home environment, Roosevelt was blessed with a sunny, optimistic outlook on life. Lincoln, in contrast, was prone to melancholy, which began to appear at an early age, when his lofty ambitions and lowly circumstances seemed totally at odds with each other.

Between Lincoln and the other Roosevelt, Theodore, we can also see a diametric opposition between their physical characteristics. Lincoln was remarkably tall, strong, athletic and healthy – qualities that brought him respect from his male companions starting from a young age. He was never sick, according to his relatives, and as a young man, he was able to carry heavy loads that would be difficult for three ordinary men to lift, according to a friend. Theodore Roosevelt, in contrast, was plagued by frequent bouts of illness, fragility and asthma that necessitated days of bed rest.

With their mental characteristics, Lincoln and Theodore Roosevelt provide another set of contrasting examples. As a child, Lincoln was praised for his exceptional feats of memory – but they did not come to him naturally. He had to put considerable effort into memorizing things – copying out whole passages from books multiple times, for instance. Roosevelt, by contrast, was blessed with a photographic memory; he could read a passage only once and remember it for the rest of his life.

Even the presidents' attitudes toward work and free time were different. Given their achievements, you might expect them all to have been workaholics, but this was true only of Johnson. He rarely saw movies or plays, almost never read anything besides the news and couldn't even attend a baseball game or a social event without turning it into an opportunity to talk about politics. In contrast, the other three presidents each had their diversions: poetry and drama for Lincoln, birds and novels for Theodore Roosevelt and sailing and poker for Franklin Roosevelt.

GREAT LEADERS HAVE DIFFERING STRENGTHS AND WEAKNESSES, WHICH ARE OFTEN LINKED.

In popular imagination, great leaders are sometimes portrayed as larger-than-life figures with almost superhuman strength. However, when we examine the transformational presidents, we see that this is an oversimplification. The presidents' were undeniably gifted, but they were also undeniably human, with strengths that were remarkable but not miraculous, and with weaknesses as well.

Let's start with their strengths. Like their circumstances and personal characteristics, these too were varied. Yet again, Lincoln and Theodore Roosevelt provide contrasting examples.

One of Lincoln's great strengths was his ability to learn through patient observation. When he first joined his state assembly, he quietly waited on the sidelines so he could watch and learn how it worked from a distance before involving himself in the fray.

Roosevelt, on the other hand, had a much more gung-ho approach: he dove right into action and aggressively interrogated his fellow legislators about how their assembly worked – often violating procedural rules and irritating his colleagues in the process.

His doing so was expressive of one of his great strengths and a potential weakness: his uncontainable energy and lack of inhibition. Like Theodore Roosevelt, Franklin Roosevelt also had a double-edged strength that could turn into a weakness. He had a willingness to bend, bypass or even break the rules when convinced that the ends justified the means.

For instance, as Assistant Secretary of the Navy, Franklin Roosevelt figured out a clever way of getting around regulations against selling weapons to merchant ships. Namely, offer them as loans instead of sales. On another occasion, he felt so certain of the need for new guns, supplies and equipment worth millions of dollars that he put in an order for them before Congress had approved the funds.

A particularly vivid illustration of a strength turning into a weakness comes from Johnson, who was masterful at using cunning procedural tactics in Congress to accomplish his agenda. For example, to rescue his civil rights bill from legislative limbo in the House of Representatives, he craftily made use of an arcane procedure known as a discharge petition, in which a bill stuck in committee was brought to the floor for a vote. However, he also used such tactics to ramp up the Vietnam War without full public awareness – by manipulating the federal budget to conceal its escalating defense costs, for instance.

AMBITION IS ONE OF THE DECISIVE FACTORS IN BECOMING A GREAT LEADER.

Despite their differences, the transformative presidents all had one thing in common: ambition.

The crucial role that ambition plays in the path to leadership can be clarified by contrasting Lincoln and Theodore Roosevelt's very different upbringings.

If you described Lincoln's impoverished, formally uneducated background on paper, he wouldn't exactly sound like he had the makings of becoming a successful politician, let alone arguably the greatest president in US history.

Thanks to his ambition, however, he was able to overcome the challenges of his upbringing and develop his talents – particularly in regard to education. We can see this even at the beginning of his educational journey. Upon learning how to print the letters of the alphabet, he started practicing his writing on every surface he could find – even charcoal, dust, sand and snow.

Fast-forward to his young adulthood, and we see the same tenacity in his independent study of the law. He would stay up late into the night after his long working day to read legal cases. He would have to borrow the law book one at a time after hiking 40 miles back and forth to get each one.

Now, cut to Theodore Roosevelt. Given his privileged upbringing, it might seem like Roosevelt had the world served to him on a silver platter and therefore didn't need ambition. But, by the same token, it would have been all too easy for him to have rested on his laurels and simply coasted into a life of comfort, especially given his frailty.

However, instead of dampening his ambition, his frailty actually helped to kindle it. Prevented from joining the physically demanding games of his siblings, Roosevelt became a voracious reader of books, which deepened his knowledge, sparked his imagination and left him with a thirst for adventure – a thirst that would later lead him to explore the backwoods of Maine and lead a regiment in the Spanish-American War.

But as long as his body remained frail, that thirst for adventure would remain unquenched. Recognizing this, he devoted himself to a strenuous exercise regime from the age of ten through college, providing himself with first-hand experience in overcoming hardship and gaining the ability to pursue many exploits later in life.

One of the crucial elements in the transformational presidents' ascendence to leadership was their abilities to combine their strengths and ambitions with a sense of greater national purpose. Lyndon Johnson clearly shows the importance of the latter, as his successes and failures largely hinged on the presence or absence of such a purpose.

One of Johnson's strengths was his mastery of clever procedural tactics. This strength could lead him to very positive accomplishments, as in his promotion of Civil Rights. However, it could also lead him to very negative results, as in his escalation of the Vietnam War.

Let's start with one of his main successes. His promotion of Civil Rights was part of his larger agenda, known as the Great Society. This referred to a set of programs aimed at eliminating not just racial injustice but also poverty. Guided by this lofty goal, he achieved an enormous amount, including the creation of a national health insurance program for the elderly, called Medicare, and the passage of the Voting Rights Act, which prohibited racially discriminatory voting laws.

Now let's turn to one of his main failures. In his escalation of the Vietnam War, he had no higher purpose guiding him. His aim was simply to avoid losing face, both personally and nationally. He thought that if North Vietnam defeated US-backed South Vietnam, it would be a humiliating blow to both his presidential legacy and America's stature in the world.

Without the guidance of a higher purpose, he went stumbling from one short-term decision to another – each one simply geared towards trying to contain the problem that the war represented. For example, in response to North Vietnamese raids on US barracks, he ordered airstrikes in February of 1965.

The airbases from which the strikes were launched needed protection, so he sent in troops to guard them. Those troops then needed protection themselves, so he sent in even more troops. By April, there were more than 50,000 US troops in South Vietnam. Eventually, that number would exceed 500,000.

Johnson's mixed legacy is a reflection of his mixed sense of higher purpose. Guided by such a purpose, he accomplished the promotion of Civil Rights and the Great Society. Lacking such a purpose, he also laid the groundwork for one of the greatest tragedies of both the '60s and the '70s: the Vietnam War – one of the most disastrous conflicts in US history.

THE PATH TO LEADERSHIP TAKES MANY TWISTS AND TURNS, WITH MAJOR SETBACKS ALONG THE WAY.

When he was 25 years old, Franklin Roosevelt envisaged a linear, step-by-step path that would take him straight to the White House – a path that combined his political ambitions with his lifelong interest in naval history. Step one, New York state legislator; step two, assistant secretary of the Navy; step three, governor of New York; step four, president of the United States.

Having achieved the first two steps by age 31, he seemed well on his way to the Oval Office. But then, the most devastating event of his life happened. At the age of 39, he developed polio, leaving him unable to walk or stand on his own.

As Franklin's story illustrates, the only certainty on the path to leadership is uncertainty. Each of the other three transformative presidents provides ample illustrations of this truth as well.

Lincoln lost his first run for office in the Illinois state assembly. After he won his second run, he staked his reputation on spearheading a push for a massive overhaul of the state's infrastructure. Facing the headwinds of a multi-year recession, the push collapsed, leaving incomplete bridges, canals and railroads in its wake.

Lincoln was so devastated by the push's failure that his friends confiscated his razors, fearing he might commit suicide. He became increasingly depressed, to the point where he became bedridden for days on end, neither eating nor sleeping, which left him emaciated and delirious. His doctors feared he was on the verge of lunacy.

Theodore Roosevelt and Johnson suffered periods of severe depression as well. For Roosevelt, it was triggered by a devastating personal loss: both his wife and his mother unexpectedly died on the same day when he was 25 years old.

For Johnson, it was precipitated by a heart attack that occurred as he was gathering steam for a presidential run after becoming the youngest ever majority leader of the US senate. With the media all but running obituaries for his political ambitions just when they seemed to be reaching their peak, he retreated to bed, laying still as a corpse in a state of despondency.

Each of the four eventual presidents found himself flat on his back, both figuratively and literally. The most pivotal moments in their paths to the White House hinged on how they got back on their feet.

*GREAT LEADERS USE CRISES AS OPPORTUNITIES TO
RETREAT, REFLECT AND REBUILD, EVENTUALLY
REEMERGING STRONGER THAN BEFORE.*

For each of the presidents, one of the most crucial steps in the path to leadership hinged on how they responded to their setbacks. For all four men, this meant retreating from politics for a while – not just to recover but also to reflect and rebuild themselves. As a result, these setbacks allowed them to forge the stronger selves that would eventually propel them to greatness.

Lincoln returned to a career as a lawyer, during which time he assiduously studied the law and developed his public speaking skills in front of juries – skills that would enable him to become one of the greatest orators in American history.

Theodore Roosevelt built a ranch in the Badlands of South Dakota and lived the life of a rugged Westerner for a couple of years – transforming his frail, boyish body into that of a muscular man and replacing his timidity with unshakable courage in the process.

Johnson withdrew to his ranch in Texas Hill Country, where he devoted six months to improving his diet, exercising, spending more time with his family, learning to treat his staff in a less demanding manner, reconnecting to his political values and reevaluating his political goals. Johnson emerged from his convalescence with a renewed sense of purpose, which led him to champion a series of boldy progressive policy proposals immediately upon his return to the Senate. These proposals included expanding Social Security and eliminating poll taxes, which were a major impediment to black citizens' abilities to vote.

Franklin Roosevelt devoted seven years to regaining his physical strength. However, his disease imposed limits on the extent to which he could recover on his own. To circumvent these limits, he gathered a small team of confidants who could act as surrogates for him – attending public events, giving speeches on his behalf and keeping his reputation alive in political circles. This small team was a harbinger of the larger teams he would assemble later when he became governor of New York and president of the United States. These teams would prove crucial to his success.

Franklin Roosevelt's restricted mobility serves as a stark reminder of the reason why every leader needs a team for support: even with Lincoln-esque mobility, no one can be everywhere or do everything at once. Everyone needs help to establish relationships and obtain information. Everyone needs strong team members to augment his or her limited powers.

This was certainly true of the transformative presidents, and it was especially true of Lincoln, who knew he needed a supportive team right from the start of his presidency. Even before his inauguration, the southern states were already seceding and forming the Confederacy, posing the gravest national crisis in the history of the United States.

To contend with this crisis, Lincoln assembled a diverse cabinet that wove together every disparate faction of his Republican Party, ranging from conservatives to radicals, and including all three of his main former rivals: Edward Bates, Salmon Chase and William Seward. With the nation in dire straits, he felt he needed to gather its most politically talented citizens to help him steer its course, regardless of their differences.

However, he derived strength from his team not just in spite of but because of its differences, which enabled him to view his decisions from multiple angles, consider alternative courses of actions and weigh his choices until the optimal ones emerged.

For example, his cabinet gave him a range of opinions on the Emancipation Proclamation, which declared the freedom of slaves living in the Confederacy. "Move forward with it right away," said some. "Hold back to avoid alienating the border states, England and

France," said others. "Be careful about the optics of issuing it now," warned his Secretary of State, William Seward, who was concerned it would seem like an act of desperation in the midst of the North's recent losses to the South.

Ultimately, Lincoln piloted a cautious middle course. He waited for a significant victory against the South before issuing the Proclamation. That victory came with the Battle of Antietam, which led to the retreat of Robert E. Lee's army from Maryland and Pennsylvania. Reflecting on the timing of the Proclamation later in life, Lincoln considered his decision to wait absolutely crucial to its success. He felt certain that if it had been issued even just six months earlier, it would have failed to find public support.

GREAT LEADERS RESPOND TO GENERAL CRISES BY LEVERAGING THE STRENGTHS THEY HAVE HONED FROM THEIR PERSONAL CRISES.

As we have seen, each of the transformative presidents faced a significant personal crisis from which they ultimately grew as leaders. Upon reaching the White House, each of them also faced a grave national crisis: for Lincoln, the Civil War; for Theodore Roosevelt, the Coal Strike of 1902; for Franklin Roosevelt, the Great Depression; and for Johnson, the assassination of President Kennedy.

Of the four presidents, Franklin Roosevelt provides the clearest illustration of the point at hand. That's in part because there were many parallels between the economic calamity behind the national crisis he faced and the physical affliction behind the personal crisis he weathered.

Like his body struck by polio, the economy was paralyzed by the Depression. Industry was grinding to a halt, and a quarter of workers were unemployed. Money stopped circulating; the banks started shutting down.

To overcome polio, Franklin had experimented with one recovery method after another – testing out dozens of newfangled contraptions, such as an electric belt and an oversized tricycle. Ultimately, he built his own rehabilitation center in Warm Springs, Georgia.

Faced with the Great Depression, he knew that a similar spirit of experimentation and willingness to pursue bold programs was needed. In both cases, he didn't know a secret solution to the problem, but he knew the only way to find one was to try things out and see what stuck.

From this spirit and willingness sprung a multitude of innovative governmental agencies designed to get people back to work, pump life back into the economy and raise the nation's spirits – programs such as the Civil Works Administration, the Works Progress Administration, the Public Works Administration and the Civilian Conservation Corps, among 16 others.

The latter was one of his first initiatives, and it set an early precedent for the boldness of his vision. Setting up 1,500 camps in America's neglected national forests, the Corps provided jobs to a quarter of a million young men at one point, who worked on clearing dead trees and shrubs, planting new trees, clearing paths and building firewalls.

His Secretary of Labor, Frances Perkins, thought the plan was a crazy pipe dream, but Roosevelt persisted, knowing all too well that desperate times called for dramatic measures.

Great leaders are not simply made by their circumstances or the personal characteristics with which they were born, nor are they lifted into their positions and accomplishments by some sort of superhuman ability to lead. They form themselves by taking their fallible strengths, fusing them with ambition and a sense of greater purpose, augmenting them with the strengths of their team members and refining them as they weather their own personal crises. By doing so, they are then able to rise to the occasion when confronted by larger crises on the world stage.

Actionable advice:

Draw leadership lessons from your own personal crises.
Like the transformational presidents, everyone has had their own "dark nights of the soul," which they've overcome in one way or another. Try asking yourself, how did you overcome yours – and how can you apply what you did then to the professional crises you may face now or in the future?

Writers Note:

If you enjoy this summary and wish to get more concise summary of more books, kindly follow the LINK below for more:

https://www.amazon.com/-/e/B07JYFMJB3

Summary of Dare to Lead by Brené Brown

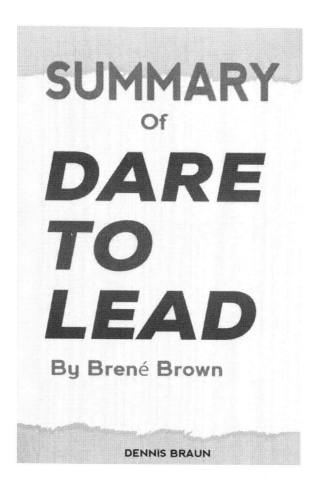

Summary of Becoming: The intimate, powerful, and inspiring memoir by the former First Lady of the United States

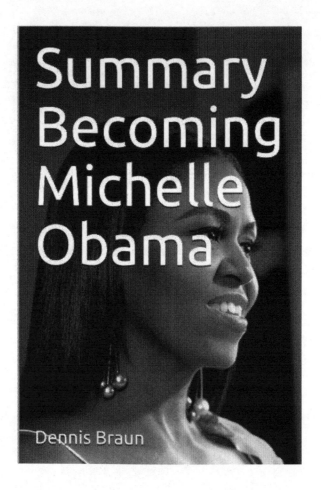

SUMMARY Fear: Trump in the White House by Bob Woodward

SUMMARY

FEAR

Trump in the White House
by BOB WOODWARD

DENNIS BRAUN

Summary of the Body Is Not an Apology: The Power of Radical Self-Love

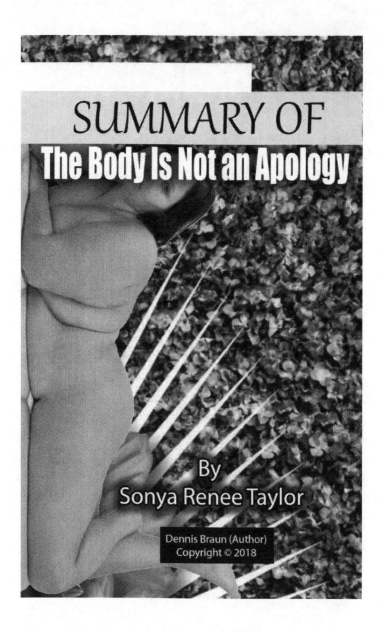

SUMMARY OF
The Body Is Not an Apology

By
Sonya Renee Taylor

Dennis Braun (Author)
Copyright © 2018

Summary of Friend of a Friend by David Burkus

SUMMARY

OF

FRIEND
—— OF A ——
FRIEND

BY DAVID BURKUS

Summary: Dambisa moyo Edge of Chaos: Why Democracy Is Failing to Deliver Economic Growth and How to Fix It

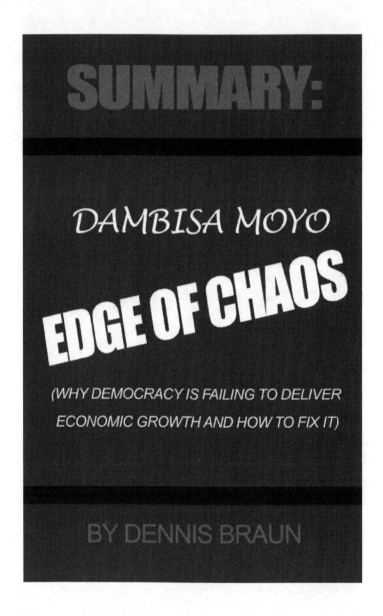

GET MORE HERE >>>

https://www.amazon.com/-/e/B07JYFMJB3

26178659R00019

Made in the USA
Lexington, KY
21 December 2018